Psychology Classics All Psychology Students Should Read:

The Bobo Doll Experiment

ALBERT BANDURA

CONTENTS

A WORD FROM THE EDITOR

Albert Bandura is one the world's most frequently cited psychologists. His ground-breaking work within the field of social learning and social cognitive theory led to a paradigm shift within psychology away from psychodynamic and behaviorist perspectives. As part of a new research agenda in the early 1960's which posited that people learn vicariously through observation Bandura began investigating aggression through imitation; work that gave rise to one of the most famous psychology studies of all time, "*Transmission of Aggression Through Imitation of Aggressive Models.*" More commonly known as "The Bobo Doll Experiment," it was the first study to explore the impact of televised violence on children.

Note To Psychology Students

If you ever have to do a paper, assignment or class project on the Bobo doll experiment having access to Bandura's original publication in full will prove invaluable. A psychology classic is by definition a must read; however, most landmark texts within the discipline remain unread by a majority of psychology students. A detailed, well written description of a classic study is fine to a point, but there is absolutely no substitute for understanding and engaging with the issues under review than by reading the authors unabridged ideas, thoughts and findings in their entirety.

As a psychology student I achieved my best grades when I was able to draw upon relevant research articles in full. When establishing your position or structuring your arguments you simply have more opportunities to reflect and pick out salient points. Being able to read a classic article in full also allows you to pick out more subtle details and issues that can be overlooked. Speaking as somebody who has graded numerous papers submitted by students on the same topic, I can tell you that these more discerning observations stand out like a beacon in the dark!

Bonus Material

Transmission of Aggression Through Imitation of Aggressive Models builds upon some of Albert Bandura's previously published work. Among the most notable of these earlier publications is Identification as a Process of Incidental Learning; which is also presented in full.

About The Editor

David Webb has a first class honors degree in psychology and a Masters in Occupational psychology. For a number of years, he was a lecturer in psychology at the University of Huddersfield (UK).

He is the writer and host of four websites built around his teaching and research interests. Together these websites receive over 120,000 unique visitors each month and generate over 4 million yearly page views.

www.all-about-psychology.com

www.all-about-forensic-psychology.com

www.all-about-forensic-science.com

www.all-about-body-language.com

An active promoter of psychology through social media his psychology facebook page (www.facebook.com/psychologyonline) has over 80,000 followers and he is listed by The British Psychological Society among the top psychologists who tweet (@psych101.)

His most recent publication, The Incredibly Interesting Psychology Book (www.amazon.com/dp/B00CR1DX22) is an international #1 Best Seller.

1. IDENTIFICATION AS A PROCESS OF INCIDENTAL LEARNING

(Albert Bandura & Aletha Huston 1961)

Although part of a child's socialization takes place through direct training much of a child's behavior repertoire is believed to be acquired through identification with the important adults in his life. This process, variously described in behavior theory as "vicarious" learning (Logan, Olmsted, Rosner, Schwartz, & Stevens, 1955), observational learning (Maccoby & Wilson, 1957; Warden, Pjeld, & Koch, 1940), and role taking (Maccoby, 1959; Sears, Maccoby, & Levin, 1957) appears to be more a result of active imitation by the child of attitudes and patterns of behavior that the parents have never directly attempted to teach than of direct reward and punishment of instrumental responses

While elaborate developmental theories have been proposed to explain this phenomenon, the process subsumed under the term "identification" may be accounted for in terms of incidental learning, that is, learning that apparently takes place in the absence of an induced set or intent to learn the specific behaviors or activities in question (McGeoch & Irion, 1952).

During the parents' social training of a child, the range of cues employed by a child is likely to include both those that the parents consider immediately relevant and other cues of parental behavior which the child has had ample opportunities to observe and to learn even though he has not been instructed to do so. Thus, for example, when a parent punishes a child physically for having aggressed toward peers, the intended outcome of the training is that the child should refrain from hitting others. Concurrent with the intentional learning, however, a certain amount of incidental learning may be expected to occur through imitation, since the child is provided, in the form of the parent's behavior, with an example of how to aggress toward others, and this incidental learning may guide the child's behavior in later social interactions.

The use of incidental cues by both human and animal subjects while performing nonimitative learning tasks is well documented by research (Easterbrook, 1959). In addition, studies of imitation and learning of incidental cues by Church (1957) and Wilson (1958) have demonstrated that subjects learn certain incidental environmental cues while imitating the discrimination behavior of a model and that the incidental learning guides the subjects' discrimination responses in the absence of the model. The purpose of the experiment reported in this paper is to demonstrate that subjects imitate not only discrimination responses but also other behaviors performed by the model.

The incidental learning paradigm was employed in the present study with an important change in procedure in order to create a situation similar to that encountered in learning through identification. Subjects performed an orienting task but, unlike most incidental learning studies, the experimenter performed the diverting task as well and the extent to which the subjects patterned their behavior after that of the experimenter-model was measured.

The main hypothesis tested is that nursery school children, while learning a two-choice discrimination problem, also learn to imitate certain of the experimenter's behaviors which are totally irrelevant to the Successful performance of the orienting task.

One may expect, on the basis of theories of identification (Bronfenbrenner, 1960), that the presence of affection and nurturance in the adult-child interaction promotes incidental imitative learning, a view to which empirical studies of the correlates of strong and weak identification lend some indirect support. Boys whose fathers are highly rewarding and affectionate have been found to adopt the father-role in doll play activities (Sears, 1953), to show father-son similarity in response to items on a personality questionnaire (Payne & Mussen. 1956), and to display masculine behaviors (Mussen & Distler, 1959, 1960) to a greater extent than boys whose fathers are relatively cold and unrewarding.

One interpretation of the relationship between nurturance and identification is that affectional rewards increase the secondary reinforcing properties of the model and, thus, predispose the imitator to reproduce the behavior of the model for the satisfaction these cues provide (Mowrer, 1950). Once the parental characteristics have acquired such reward value for the child, conditional withdrawal of positive reinforcers is believed to create additional instigation for the child to perform behaviors resembling that of the parent model i.e., if the child can reproduce the parent's rewarding behavior he can, thus, reward himself (Sears, 1957; Whiting & Child, 1953). In line with this theory of identification in term of secondary reward, it is predicted that children who experience a warm, rewarding interaction with the experimenter-model should reproduce significantly more of the behaviors performed by the model than do children who experience a relatively distant and cold relationship.

METHOD

Subjects

The subjects were 24 boys and 24 girls enrolled in the Stanford University Nursery School. They ranged in age from 45 to 61 months, with a mean age of 53 months. The junior author played the role of the model for all 48 children, and two other female experimenters shared in the task of conducting the study.

General Procedure

Forty subjects mere matched individually on the basis of sex and ratings of dependency behavior, and subdivided randomly in terms of a nurturant-non nurturant condition yielding two experimental groups of 20 subjects each. A small control group comprising 8 subjects was also studied.

In the first phase of the experiment half the experimental and control subjects experienced two nurturant rewarding play sessions with the model while the remaining subjects experienced a cold nonnurturant relationship. For the second phase of the experiment subjects performed a diverting two-choice discrimination problem with the model who exhibited fairly explicit, although functionless behavior during the discrimination trials, and the extent to which the subjects reproduced the model's behavior was measured. The experimental and control procedures differed only in the patterns of behavior displayed by the model.

Matching Variable

Dependency was selected as a matching variable since, on the basis of the theories of identification dependency would be expected to facilitate imitative learning. There is some evidence, for example, that dependent subjects are strongly oriented toward gaining social rewards in the form of attention and approval (Cairns, 1959; Endsley & Hartup, 1960), and one means of obtaining these rewards is to imitate behavior of others (Sears, Maccoby, & Levin, 1957). Moreover, such children do not have the habit of responding independently; consequently they are apt to be more dependent on, and therefore more attentive to, the cues produced by the behavior of others (Jackubczak & Walters, 1959; Kagan & Mussen, 1956).

Measures of subjects' dependency behavior were obtained through observations of their social interactions in the nursery school. The observers recorded subjects' behavior using a combined time-sampling and behavior unit observation method. Each child was observed for 12 10-minute observation sessions distributed over a period of approximately 10 weeks; each observation session was divided into 30-second intervals, thus yielding a total of 240 behavior units.

The children were observed in a predetermined order that was varied randomly to insure that each child would be seen under approximately comparable conditions. In order to provide an estimate of reliability of the ratings, 234 observation sessions (4,680 behavior units) were recorded simultaneously but independently by both observers.

The subjects emotional dependency was assessed in terms of the frequency of behaviors that were aimed at securing a nurturant response from others. The following four specific categories of dependency behavior were scored: seeking help and assistance, seeking praise and approval, seeking physical contact and seeking proximity and company of others.

The dependency scores were obtained by summing the observations made of these five different type behaviors and, on the basis of these scores, the subjects were paired and assigned at random to the two experimental conditions.

Experimental Conditions

In the nonnurturant condition, the model brought the subject to the experimental room and after instructing the child to play with the toys that were spread on the floor, busied herself with paper work at a desk in the far corner of the room. During this period the model avoided any interaction with the child.

In contrast, during the nurturant sessions the model sat on the floor close to the subject. She responded readily to the child's bids for help and attention, and in other ways fostered a consistently warm, and rewarding interaction.

These experimental social interactions, which preceded the imitation learning, consisted of two 15-minute sessions separated by an interval of approximately 5 days.

Diverting Task

A two-choice discrimination problem, similar to the one employed by Miller and Dollard (1941) in experiments of matching behavior, was used as the diverting task which occupied the subjects' attention while at the same time permitting opportunities for the subjects to observe behavior performed by the model in the absence of any instructions to observe or to reproduce the responses resembling that of the model.

The apparatus consisted of two small boxes, identical in color (red sides, yellow lid) and size (6" X 8" X 10"). The hinged lid of each box was lined with rubber stripping so as to eliminate any auditory cues during the placement of the rewards which consisted of small multicolor pictures of animals and flowers. The boxes were placed on small chairs approximately 5 feet apart and 8 feet from the starting point.

At the end of the second social interaction session the experimenter entered the room with the test apparatus and instructed the model and the subject that they were going to play a game in which the experimenter would hide a picture sticker in one of the boxes and that the object of the game was to guess which box contained the sticker.

The model and the subject then left the room and after the experimenter placed two stickers in the designated box, they were recalled to the starting point in the experimental room and the model was asked to take the first turn. During the model's trial, the subject remained at the starting point where he could observe the model's behavior.

Although initially it was planned to follow the procedure used by Miller and Dollard (1941) in which one of two boxes was loaded with two rewards and the child made his choice immediately following the leader's trial, this procedure had to be modified when it became evident during pretesting that approximately 40% of the subjects invariably chose the opposite box from the model even though the nonimitative response was consistently unrewarded. McDavid (1959), in a recent study of imitative behavior in preschool children, encountered similar difficulties in that 44% of his subjects did not learn to imitate the leader even though the subjects were not informed as to whether the leader was or was not rewarded.

In order to overcome this stereotyped nonimitation, the experimenter placed two rewards in a single box, but following the model's trial the model and the subject left the room and were recalled almost immediately (the intratrial interval was approximately 5 seconds), thus, creating the impression that the boxes were reloaded. After the subject completed his trial, the model and the subject left the room. The experimenter recorded the subject's behavior and reloaded the boxes for the second trial. The noncorrection method was used throughout. This procedure was continued until the subject met the learning criterion of four successive imitative discrimination responses, or until 30 acquisition trials had been completed. The slight modification in procedure proved to be effective as evidenced by the fact that only 9 of the 48 children failed to meet the criterion.

In order to eliminate any position habit, the right-left placements of the reward were varied from trial to trial in a fixed irregular order. This sequence was randomly determined except for the limitation that no more than two successive rewards could occur in the same position.

The number of trials to criterion was the measure of the subjects' imitation behavior on the discrimination task.

Although the establishment of imitative choice responses was, in itself, of some theoretical interest, the discrimination problem was intended primarily as an orienting or distraction task. Thus, on each discrimination trial, the model exhibited certain verbal, motor, and aggressive behaviors which were totally irrelevant to the performance of the task to which the subject's attention was directed. At the starting point, for example, the model remarked, "Here I go," and then marched slowly toward the box containing the stickers repeating, "March, march, march." On the lid of each box was a small rubber doll which the model knocked off aggressively when she reached the designated box. She then paused briefly, remarked, "Open the box," removed one sticker and pasted it on a pastoral scene that hung on the wall immediately behind the boxes. The model terminated the trial by replacing the doll on the lid of the container. The model and the subject then left the room briefly. After being recalled to the experimental room the subject took his turn, and the number of the model's behaviors reproduced by the subject was recorded.

Control Group

In addition to the two experimental groups, a control group, consisting of eight subjects, comparable to the experimental groups in terms of sex distribution, dependency ratings, and nurturant-nonnurturant experiences was studied. Since the model performed highly novel patterns of responses unlikely to occur independently of the observation of the behavior of the model, it was decided to assign most of the available subjects to the experimental groups and only a small number of subjects to the control group.

The reasons for the inclusion of a control group were twofold. On the one hand, it provided a check on whether the subjects' behavior reflected genuine imitative learning or merely the chance occurrence of behaviors high in the subjects' response hierarchies. Second, it was of interest to determine whether the subjects would adopt certain aspects of the model's behavior that involved considerable delay in reward. With the controls, therefore, the model walked to the box, choosing a highly circuitous route along the sides of the experimental room; instead of aggressing toward the doll, the model lifted it gently off the container and she left the doll on the floor at the completion of a trial. While walking to the boxes the model repeated, "Walk, walk, walk."

Imitation Scores

On each trial the subjects' performances were scored in terms of the following imitation response categories: selects box chosen by the model; marches; repeats the phrases, "Here I go," "March, march," "Open box," or "Walk, walk"; aggresses toward the doll; replaces doll on box; imitates the circuitous route to the box.

Some subjects made a verbal response in the appropriate context (for example, at the starting point, on the way to the box, before raising the lid of the container) but did not repeat the model's exact words. These verbal responses were also scored and interpreted as partially imitative behavior.

In order to provide an estimate of the reliability of the experimenter's scoring the performances of 19 subjects were scored independently by two judges who alternated in observing the experimental sessions through a one-way mirror from an adjoining observation room.

RESULTS

Reliability of Observations of Dependency Behavior

The reliability of the observers' behavior ratings was estimated by means of an index of agreement based on the ratio of twice the number of agreements over the combined ratings of the two observers multiplied by 100. Since small time discrepancies, due to inevitable slight asynchronism of the observers' timing devices, were expected, a time discrepancy in rating a given behavior category greater than two 30-second intervals was interpreted as a disagreement.

The interobserver reliabilities for the dependency categories considered separately were as follows: Positive attention seeking, 84%; help seeking, 72%; seeking physical contact, 84%; and seeking proximity, 75%.

Reliability of Imitation Scores

The percentage of agreement in scoring imitative behavior in the experimental sessions is presented below.

Aggression 98%

Marching 73%

Imitative Verbal Behavior 80%

Partially Imitative Verbal Behavior 83%

Other Imitative Responses 50%

Replaces Doll 99%

Circuitous Route 96%

Except for other imitative responses, the subjects' behavior was scored with high reliability and, even in the letter response category, the scoring discrepancies arose primarily from the experimenter's lack of opportunity to observe some of the behaviors in question rather than from differences of interpretation, for example when the subject made appropriate mouth movements but emitted no sound while marching toward the containers, this partial imitation of the model's verbalizations could not be readily observed by the experimenter (who was at the starting point) but was clearly evident to the rater in the observation room.

Incidental Initiation of Model's Behavior

Since the data disclosed no significant sex differences, the imitation scores for the male and female subgroups were combined in the statistical analyses.

Ninety percent of the subjects in the experimental groups adopted the model's aggressive behavior, 45 % imitated the marching, and 28% reproduced the model's verbalizations. In contrast, none of the control subjects behaved aggressively, marched or verbalized, while 75 % of the controls and none of the experimental subjects imitated the circuitous route to the containers. Except for replacing the doll on the box, which was performed by most of the experimental and control subjects, there was no overlap in the imitative behavior displayed by the two groups.

While the control subjects replaced the doll on the box slightly more often than the subjects in the experimental group, this difference tested by means of the median test was not statistically significant ($x2 = 1.49$; $df = 1$). Evidently the response of replacing things, undoubtedly overtrained by parents, is so well established that it occurs independently of the behavior of the model. Since this was clearly a nonimitative response, it was not included in the subsequent analyses.

To the extent that behavior of the sort evoked in this study may be considered an elementary prototype of identification, the results add support to the interpretation of identification as a process of incidental imitative learning.

Effects of Nurturance on Imitation

In order to make comparable the imitation scores for the subjects who varied somewhat in the number of trials to criterion, the total imitative responses in a given response category were divided by the number of trials. Since only a small number of subjects in the nonnurturant condition displayed imitative nonaggressive behavior and the distributions of scores were markedly skewed, the sign test was used to estimate the significance of differences between the two experimental groups.

The predicted facilitating effect of social rewards on imitation was essentially confirmed. Subjects who experienced the rewarding interaction with the model marched and verbalized imitatively, and reproduced other responses resembling that of the model to a greater extent than did the subjects who experienced the relatively cold and distant relationship. Aggression, interestingly, was readily imitated by subjects regardless of the quality of the model-child relationship.

Imitation of Discrimination Responses

A three-way analysis of variance (McNemar, 1955, Case XVII) of the trials scores failed to show any significant effects of nurturance or sex of imitator on the imitation of discrimination responses, nor did the two groups or experimental subjects differ significantly in the number of trials in which they imitated the model's choice or in the number of trials to the first imitative discrimination response.

While nurturance did not seem to influence the actual choices the subjects made, it nevertheless affected their predecision behavior. A number of the children displayed considerable conflictful vacillation, often running back and forth between the boxes, prior to making their choice. In the analysis of these data, the vacillation scores were divided by the total number of trials, and the significance of the differences was estimated by means of the sign test since the distribution of scores was markedly skewed. The results of this test revealed that the subjects in the nurturant condition exhibited more conflictful behavior than subjects in the nonnurturant group (p = .03). This finding is particularly noteworthy considering that one has to counteract a strong nonimitation bias in getting preschool children to follow a leader in a two-choice discrimination problem as evidenced by McDavid's (1959) findings as well as those of the present study (i.e., 75% of the subjects made nonimitative choices on the first trial).

Dependency and Imitation

Correlations between the ratings of dependency behavior and the measures of imitation were calculated separately for the nurturant and nonnurturant experimental subgroups, and where the correlation coefficients did not differ significantly the data were combined. The expected positive relationship between dependency and imitation was only partially supported. High dependent subjects expressed more partially imitative verbal behavior ($rt = .60$; $p < .05$) and exhibited more predecision conflict on the discrimination task ($r = .26$; $p = .05$) than did subjects who were rated low on dependency.

Dependency and total imitation of nonaggressive responses was positively related for boys ($rt = .31$) but negatively correlated for girls ($rt = -.46$). These correlations, however, are not statistically significant. Nor was there any significant relationship between dependency and imitation of aggression ($r = .20$) or discrimination responses ($r = -.03$).

DISCUSSION

The results of this study generally substantiate the hypotheses that children display a good deal of social learning of an incidental imitative sort, and that nurturance is one condition facilitating such imitative learning.

The extent to which the model's behavior had come to influence and control the behavior of subjects is well illustrated by their marching, and by their choice of the circuitous route to the containers. Evidence from the pretesting and from the subjects' behavior during the early discrimination trials revealed that dashing toward the boxes was the dominant response, and that the delay produced by marching or by taking an indirect route that more than doubled the distance to the boxes was clearly incompatible with the subjects' eagerness to get to the containers. Nevertheless, many subjects dutifully followed the example set by the model.

Even more striking was the subjects' imitation of responses performed unwittingly by the model. On one trial with a control

13

subject, for example, the model began to replace the doll on the box at the completion of the trial when suddenly, startled by the realization of the mistake, she quickly replaced the doll on the floor. Sure enough, on the next trial, the subject took the circuitous route, removed the doll gently off the box and, after disposing of the sticker, raised the doll, and then quickly replaced it on the floor reproducing the model's startled reaction as well!

The results for the influence of nurturance on imitation of verbal behavior are in accord with Mower's (1950) autism theory of word learning. Moreover, the obtained significant effect of nurturance on the production of partially imitative verbal responses indicates that nurturance not only facilitates imitation of the specific behaviors displayed by a model but also increases the probability of responses of a whole response class (for example, verbal behavior). These data are essentially in agreement with those of Milner (1951), who found that mothers of children receiving high reading readiness scores were more verbal and affectionately demonstrative in the interactions with their children than were the mothers of subjects in the low reading ability group.

That the incidental cues of the model's behavior may have taken on positive valence and were consequently reproduced by subjects for the mere satisfaction of performing them, is suggested by the fact that children in the nurturant condition not only marched to the containers but also marched in and out of the experimental room and marched about in the anteroom repeating, "March, march, march," etc., while waiting for the next trial. While certain personality patterns may be, thus, incidentally acquired, the stability and persistence of these behaviors in the absence of direct rewards by external agents remains to be studied.

A response cannot be readily imitated unless its components are within the subjects behavior repertoire. The fact that gross motor responses are usually more highly developed than verbal skills in

14

young children may explain why subjects reproduced the model's marching (p = .05) and aggression (p < .001) to a significantly greater extent than they did her verbal behavior. Indeed several subjects imitated the motor component of speech by performing the appropriate mouth movements but emitted no sound. The greater saliency of the model's motor responses might also be a possible explanation of the obtained differences.

"Identification with the aggressor" (Freud, 1937) or "defensive identification" (Mowrer, 1950), whereby a child presumably transforms himself from object to agent of aggression by adopting the attributes of an aggressive, punitive model so as to allay anxiety, is widely accepted as an explanation of the imitative learning of aggression. The results of the present study, and those of a second experiment now in progress, suggest that the mere observation of aggressive models, regardless of the quality of the model-child relationship, is a sufficient condition for producing imitative aggression in children. A comparative study of subjects' imitation of aggressive models who are feared, who are liked and esteemed, or who are more or less neutral figures would throw some light on whether or not a more parsimonious theory than the one involved in "identification with the aggressor" can explain the modeling process.

Although the results from the present study provide evidence that nurturance promotes incidental imitative learning, the combination of nurturance followed by its withdrawal would be expected, according to the secondary reinforcement theory of imitation, to furnish stronger incentive than nurturance alone for subjects to reproduce a model's behavior. It is also possible that dependency may be essentially unrelated to imitation under conditions of consistent nurturance, but may emerge as a variable facilitating imitation under conditions where social reinforcers are temporarily withdrawn.

The experiment reported in this paper focused on immediate imitation in the presence of the model. A more crucial test of the transmission of behavior through the process of social imitation involves the generalization of imitative responses to new situations in which the model is absent. A study of this type, involving the delayed imitation of both male and female aggressive models, is currently under way.

SUMMARY

The present study was primarily designed to test the hypotheses that children would learn to imitate behavior exhibited by an experimenter-model, and that a nurturant interaction between the model and the child would enhance the secondary reward properties of the model and thus facilitate such imitative learning.

Forty-eight preschool children performed a diverting two-choice discrimination problem with a model who displayed fairly explicit, although functionless, behaviors during the trials. With the experimental subjects the model marched, emitted specific verbal responses, and aggressed toward dolls located on the discrimination boxes; with the controls the model walked to the boxes choosing a highly circuitous route and behaved in a nonaggressive fashion. Half the subjects in the experimental and control groups experienced a rewarding interaction with the model prior to the imitative learning while the remaining subjects experienced a cold and nonnurturant relationship.

The following results were obtained:

1. The experimental and the control subjects not only reproduced behaviors resembling that of their model but also, except for one response category, did not overlap in the types of imitative responses they displayed.

2. The predicted facilitating effect of social rewards on imitation was also confirmed, the only exception being for aggression, which was readily imitated by the subjects regardless of the quality of the model-

child relationship.

3. Although nurturance was not found to influence the rate of imitative discrimination learning, subjects in the nurturant condition exhibited significantly more predecision conflict behavior than did subjects in the nonnurturant group.

REFERENCES

BRONFENBRENNER, U. Freudian theories of identification and their derivatives. Child Develpm., 1960, 31, 15-40.

CAIRNS, R. B, The influence of dependency-anxiety on the effectiveness of social reinforcers. Unpublished doctoral dissertation, Stanford University, 1959.

CHURCH, R. M. Transmission of learned behavior between rats. J. abnorm. soc. Psychol., 1957, 54, 163-165.

EASTERBROOK, J. A. The effect of emotion on cue utilization and the organization of behavior. Psychol. Rev., 1959, 66, 183-201.

ENDSLEY, R. C., & HARTUP, W. W. Dependency and performance by preschool children on a socially reinforced task. Amer. Psychologist, 1960, 16, 399. (Abstract)

FREUD, ANNA. The ego and the mechanisms of defence. London: Hogarth, 1937.

JACKUBCZAK, L. F., & WALTERS, R. H. Suggestibility as dependency behavior. J. abnorm. soc. Psychol., 1959, 59, 102-107.

KAGAN, J., & MUSSEN, P. H. Dependency themes on the TAT and group conformity. J. consult. Psychol., 1956, 20, 29-32.

LOGAN, F., OLMSTED, D. L., ROSNER, B. S., SCHWARTZ, R. D., & STEVENS, C. M. Behavior theory and social science. New Haven: Yale Univer. Press, 1955.

MACCOBY, ELEANOR E. Role-taking in childhood and its consequences for social learning. Child Develpm., 1959, 30, 239-252.

MACCOBY, ELEANOR E., & WILSON, W, C. Identification and observational learning from films. J. abnorm. soc. Psychol., 1957, 55, 76-87.

McDAViD, J. W. Imitative behavior in preschool children. Psychol. Monogr., 1959, 73(16, Whole No. 486).

McGEOCH, J. A., & IRION, A. L. The psychology of human learning. New York: Longmans, Green, 1952.

McNEMAR, Q. Psychological statistics. New York: Wiley, 1955.

MILLER, N. E., & DOLLARD, J. Social learning and imitation. New Haven: Yale Univer. Press, 1941.

MILNER, ESTHER. A study of the relationship between reading readiness and patterns of parent-child interaction. Child Develpm., 1951, 22, 95-112.

MOWRER, O. H. Identification: A link between learning theory and psychotherapy. In, Learning theory and personality dynamics. New York: Ronald, 1950. Pp. 573-616.

MUSSEN, P., & DISTLER, L. M. Masculinity, identification, and father-son relationships. J. abnorm. soc. Psychol, 1959, 59, 350-356.

MUSSEN, P., & DISTLER, L. M. Child-rearing antecedents of masculine identification in kindergarten boys. Child Develpm., 1960, 31, 89-100.

PAYNE, D. E., & MUSSEN, P. H. Parent-child relationships and father identification among adolescent boys. J. abnorm. soc. Psychol., 1956, 52, 358-362.

SEARS, PAULINE S. Child-rearing factors related to playing of sex-typed roles. Amer. Psychologist, 1953, 8, 431. (Abstract)

SEARS, R. R. Identification as a form of behavioral development. In D. B. Harris (Ed.), The concept of development. Minneapolis: Univer. Minnesota Press, 1957. Pp. 149-161.

SEARS, R. R., MACCOBY, ELEANOR E., & LEVIN, H. Patterns of child rearing. Evanston: Row, Peterson, 1957.

WARDEN, C. J,, FJELD, H. A., & KOCH, A. M. Imitative behavior in cebus and rhesus monkeys. J. genet. Psychol., 1940, 66, 311-322.

WHITING, J. W. M., & CHILD, I. L. Child training and personality. New Haven: Yale Univer. Press, 1953.

WILSON, W. C. Imitation and learning of incidental cues by preschool children. Child Develpm., 1958, 29, 393-397.

2. TRANSMISSION OF AGGRESSION THROUGH IMITATION OF AGGRESSIVE MODELS

(Albert Bandura, Dorothea Ross & Sheila A. Ross (1961))

A previous study, designed to account for the phenomenon of identification in terms of incidental learning, demonstrated that children readily imitated behavior exhibited by an adult model in the presence of the model (Bandura & Huston, 1961). A series of experiments by Blake (1958) and others (Grosser, Polansky, & Lippitt, 1951; Rosenblith, 1959; Schachter & Hall, 1952) have likewise shown that mere observation responses of a model has a facilitating effect on subjects' reactions in the immediate social influence setting. While these studies provide convincing evidence for the influence and control exerted on others by the behavior of a model, a more crucial test of imitative learning involves the generalization of imitative response patterns new settings in which the model is absent.

In the experiment reported in this paper children were exposed to aggressive and nonaggressive adult models and were then tested amount of imitative learning in a new situation on in the absence of the model. According the prediction, subjects exposed to aggressive models would reproduce aggressive acts resembling those of their models and would differ in this respect both from subjects who served nonaggressive models and from those who had no prior exposure to any models. This hypothesis assumed that subjects had learned imitative habits as a result of prior reinforcement, and these tendencies would generalize to some extent to adult experimenters (Miller & Dollard, 1941).

It was further predicted that observation of subdued nonaggressive models would have generalized inhibiting effect on the subjects' subsequent behavior, and this effect would be reflected in a difference between the nonaggressive and the control groups, with subjects in the latter group displaying significantly more aggression.

Hypotheses were also advanced concerning the influence of the sex of model and sex of subjects on imitation. Fauls and Smith (1956) have shown that preschool children perceive their parents as having distinct preferences regarding sex appropriate modes of behavior for their children. Their findings, as well as informal observation, suggest that parents reward imitation of sex appropriate behavior and discourage or punish sex inappropriate imitative responses, e.g., a male child is unlikely to receive much reward for performing female appropriate activities, such as cooking, or for adopting other aspects of the maternal role, but these same behaviors are typically welcomed if performed by females. As a result of differing reinforcement histories, tendencies to imitate male and female models thus acquire differential habit strength. One would expect, on this basis, subjects to imitate the behavior of a same-sex model to a greater degree than a model of the opposite sex.

Since aggression, however, is a highly masculine-typed behavior, boys should be more predisposed than girls toward imitating aggression, the difference being most marked for subjects exposed to the male aggressive model.

METHOD

Subjects

The subjects were 36 boys and 36 girls enrolled in the Stanford University Nursery' School. They ranged in age from 37 to 69 months, with a mean age of 52 months.

Two adults, a male and a female, served in the role of model, and one female experimenter conducted the study for all 72 children.

Experimental Design

Subjects were divided into eight experimental groups of six subjects each and a control group consisting of 24 subjects. Half the experimental subjects were exposed to aggressive models and half were exposed to models that were subdued and nonaggressive in their behavior. These groups were further subdivided into male and female subjects. Half the subjects in the aggressive and nonaggressive conditions observed same-sex models, while the remaining subjects in each group viewed models of the opposite sex. The control group had no prior exposure to the adult models and was tested only in the generalization situation.

It seemed reasonable to expect that the subjects' level of aggressiveness would be positively related to the readiness with which they imitated aggressive modes of behavior. Therefore, in order to increase the precision of treatment comparisons, subjects in the experimental and control groups were matched individually on the basis of ratings of their aggressive behavior in social interactions in the nursery school.

The subjects were rated on four five-point rating scales by the experimenter and a nursery school teacher, both of whom were well acquainted with the children. These scales measured the extent to which subjects displayed physical aggression, verbal aggression, aggression toward inanimate objects, and aggressive inhibition. The latter scale, which dealt with the subjects' tendency to inhibit aggressive reactions in the face of high instigation, provided a measure of aggression anxiety.

Fifty-one subjects were rated independently by both judges so as to permit an assessment of interrater agreement. The reliability of the composite aggression score, estimated by means of the Pearson product-moment correlation, was .89.

The composite score was obtained by summing the ratings on the four aggression scales; on the basis of these scores, subjects were arranged in triplets and assigned at random to one of two treatment conditions or to the control group.

Experimental Conditions

In the first step in the procedure subjects were brought individually by the experimenter to the experimental room and the model who was in the hallway outside the room, was invited by the experimenter to come and join in the game. The experimenter then escorted the subject to one corner of the room, which was structured as the subject's play area. After seating the child at a small table, the experimenter demonstrated how the subject could design pictures with potato prints and picture stickers provided. The potato prints included a variety of geometrical forms; the stickers were attractive multicolor pictures of animals, flowers, and Western figures to be pasted on a pastoral scene. These activities were selected since they had been established, by previous studies in the nursery school, as having high interest value for the children.

After having settled the subject in his corner, the experimenter escorted the model to the opposite corner of the room which contained a small table and chair, a tinker toy set, a mallet, and a 5-foot inflated Bobo doll. The experimenter explained that these were the materials provided for the model to play with and, after the model was seated, the experimenter left the experimental room.

With subjects in the nonaggressive condition, the model assembled the tinker toys in a quiet subdued manner totally ignoring the Bobo doll. In contrast, with subjects in the aggressive condition, the model began by assembling the tinker toys but after approximately a minute had elapsed, the model turned to the Bobo doll and spent the remainder of the period aggressing toward it.

Imitative learning can be clearly demonstrated if a model performs sufficiently novel patterns of responses which are unlikely to occur independently of the observation of the behavior of a model and if a subject reproduces these behaviors in substantially identical form. For this reason, in addition to punching the Bobo doll, a response that is likely to be performed be children independently of a demonstration, the model exhibited distinctive aggressive acts which were to be scored as imitative responses. The model laid the Bobo doll on its side, sat on it and punched it repeatedly in the nose. The model then raised the Bobo doll, pick up the mallet and struck the doll on the head. Following the mallet aggression, the model tossed the doll up in the air aggressively and kicked it about the room. This sequence of physically aggressive acts was repeated approximately three times, interspersed with verbally aggressive responses such as, "Sock him in the nose...," "Hit him down...," "Throw him in the air...," "Kick him...," "Pow...," and two non-aggressive comments, "He keeps coming back for more" and "He sure is a tough fella."

Thus in the exposure situation, subjects were provided with a diverting task which occupied their attention while at the same time insured observation of the model's behavior in the absence of any instructions to observe or to learn the responses in question. Since subjects could not perform the model's aggressive behavior, any learning that occurred was purely on an observational or covert basis.

At the end of 10 minutes, the experimenter entered the room, informed the subject that he would now go to another game room, and bid the model goodbye.

Aggression Arousal

Subjects were tested for the amount of imitative learning in a different experimental room that was set off from the main nursery school building, The two experimental situations were thus clearly differentiated; in fact, many subjects were under the impression that they were no longer on the nursery school grounds.

Prior to the test for imitation, however, all subjects, experimental and control, were subjected to mild aggression arousal to insure that they were under some degree of instigation to aggression. The arousal experience was included for two main reasons. In the first place, observation of aggressive behavior exhibited by others tends to reduce the probability of aggression on the part of the observer (Rosenbaum & deCharms, 1960). Consequently, subjects in the aggressive condition, in relation both to the nonaggressive and control groups, would he under weaker instigation following exposure to the models. Second, if subjects in the nonaggressive condition expressed little aggression in the face of appropriate instigation, the presence of an inhibitory process would seem to be indicated.

Following the exposure experience, therefore, the experimenter brought the subject to an anteroom that contained these relatively attractive toys: a fire engine, a locomotive, a jet fighter plane, a cable car, a colorful spinning top, and a doll set complete with wardrobe, doll carriage, and baby crib. The experimenter explained that the toys were for the subject to play with but, as soon as the subject became sufficiently involved with the play material (usually in about 2 minutes), the experimenter remarked that these were her very best toys, that she did not let just anyone play with them, and that she had decided to reserve these toys for the other children. However, the subject could play with any of the toys that were in the next room. The experimenter and the subject then entered the adjoining experimental room.

It was necessary for the experimenter to remain in the room during the experimental session; otherwise a number of the children would either refuse to remain alone or would leave before the termination of the session. However, in order to minimize any influence her presence might have on the subject's behavior, the experimenter remained as inconspicuous as possible by busying herself with paper work at a desk in the far corner of the room and avoiding any interaction with the child.

Test For Delayed Imitation

The experimental room contained a variety of toys including some that could be used in imitative or nonimitative aggression, and others that tended to elicit predominantly nonaggressive forms of behavior. The aggressive toys included a 3-foot Bobo doll, a mallet and peg board, two dart guns, and a tether ball with a face painted on it which hung from the ceiling. The nonaggressive toys, on the other hand, included a tea set, crayons and coloring paper, a ball, two dolls, three bears, cars and trucks, and plastic farm animals. The experimental room contained a variety of toys including some that could be used in imitative or nonimitative aggression, and others that tended to elicit predominantly nonaggressive forms of behavior. The aggressive toys included a 3-foot Bobo doll, a mallet and peg board, two dart guns, and a tether ball with a face painted on it which hung from the ceiling. The nonaggressive toys, on the other hand, included a tea set, crayons and coloring paper, a ball, two dolls, three bears, cars and trucks, and plastic farm animals.

The subject spent 20 minutes in this experiments room during which time his behavior was rated in terms of predetermined response categories by judges who observed the session though a one-way mirror in an adjoining observation room. The 20 minute session was divided into 5-second intervals by means of at electric interval timer, thus yielding a total number of 240 response units for each subject.

The male model scored the experimental sessions for all 72 children. Except for the cases in which he, served as the model, he did not have knowledge of the subjects' group assignments. In order to provide an estimate of interscorer agreement, the performance of half the subjects were also scored independently by second observer. Thus one or the other of the two observers usually had no knowledge of the conditions to which the subjects were assigned. Since, however, all but two of the subjects in the aggressive condition performed the models' novel aggressive responses while subjects in the other conditions only rarely exhibited such reactions, subjects who were exposed to the aggressive models could be readily identified through the distinctive behavior.

The responses scored involved highly specific concrete classes of behavior and yielded high interscorer reliabilities, the product-moment coefficients being in the .90s.

Response Measures

Three measures of imitation were obtained:

Imitation of physical aggression: This category included acts of striking the Bobo doll with the mallet, sitting on the doll and punching it in the nose, kicking the doll, and tossing it in the air.

Imitative verbal aggression: Subject repeats the phrases, "Sock him," "Hit him down," "Kick him," "Throw him in the air," or "Pow"

Imitative nonaggressive verbal responses: Subject repeats, "He keeps coming back for more," or "He sure is a tough fella."

During the pretest, a number of the subjects imitated the essential components of the model's behavior but did not perform the complete act, or they directed the imitative aggressive response to some object other than the Bobo doll. Two responses of this type were therefore scored and were interpreted as partially imitative behavior.

Mallet aggression: Subject strikes objects other than the Bobo doll aggressively with the mallet.

Sits on Bobo doll: Subject lays the Bobo doll on its side and sits on it, but does not aggress toward it.

The following additional nonimitative aggressive responses were scored:

Punches Bobo doll: Subject strikes, slaps, or pushes the doll aggressively.

Nonimitative physical and verbal aggression: This category included physically aggressive acts directed toward objects other than the Bubo doll and any hostile remarks except for those in the verbal imitation category; e.g., "Shoot the Bobo," "Cut him," "Stupid ball," "Knock over people," "Horses fighting, biting"

Aggressive gun play: Subject shoots darts or aims the guns and fires imaginary shots at objects in the room.

Ratings were also made of the number of behavior units in which subjects played nonaggressively or sat quietly and did not play with any of the material at all.

RESULTS

Complete Imitation of Models' Behavior

Subjects in the aggression condition reproduced a good deal of physical and verbal aggressive behavior resembling that of the models, and their mean scores differed markedly from those of subjects in the nonaggressive and control groups who exhibited virtually no imitative aggression.

Since there were only a few scores for subjects in the nonaggressive and control conditions (approximately 70% of the subjects had zero scores), and the assumption of homogeneity of variance could not be made, the Friedman two-way analysis of variance by ranks was employed to test the significance of the obtained differences.

The prediction that exposure of subjects to aggressive models increases the probability of aggressive behavior is clearly confirmed. The main effect of treatment conditions is highly significant both for physical and verbal imitative aggression. Comparison of pairs of scores by the sign test shows that the obtained over-all differences were due almost entirely to the aggression displayed by subjects who had been exposed to the aggressive models. Their scores were significantly higher than those of either the nonaggressive or control groups, which did not differ from each other.

Imitation was not confined to the model's aggressive responses. Approximately one-third of the subjects in the aggressive condition also repeated the model's nonaggressive verbal responses while none of the subjects in either the nonaggressive or control groups made such remarks. This difference, tested by means of the Cochran Q test, was significant well beyond the .001 level.

Partial Imitation of Models' Behavior

Differences in the predicted direction were also obtained on the two measures of partial imitation. Analysis of variance of scores based on the subjects' use of the mallet aggressively toward objects other than the Bobo doll reveals that treatment conditions are a statistically significant source of variation. In addition, individual sign tests show that both the aggressive and the control groups, relative to subjects in the nonaggressive condition, produced significantly more mallet aggression, the difference being particularly marked with regard to female subjects. Girls who observed nonaggressive model performed a mean number of 0.5 mallet aggression responses as compared to mean values of 18.0 and 13.1 for girls in the aggressive and control groups, respectively.

Although subjects who observed aggressive models performed more mallet aggression (M = 20.0) than their controls (M = 13.3), the difference was not statistically significant.

With respect to the partially imitative response of sitting on the Bobo doll, the over-all group differences were significantly beyond the .01 level. Comparison of pairs of scores by the sign test procedure reveals that subjects in the aggressive group reproduced this aspect of the models' behavior to a greater extent than did the nonaggressive (p

= .018) or the control (p = .059) subjects. The latter two groups, on the other hand, did not differ from each other.

Nonimitative Aggression

Analyses of variance of the remaining aggression measures show that treatment conditions did not influence the extent to which subjects engaged in aggressive gun play or punched the Bobo doll. The effect of conditions is highly significant (c 2r = 8.96, p < .02), however in the case of the subjects' expression of nonimitative physical and verbal aggression. Further comparison of treatment pairs reveals that the main source of the over-all difference was the aggressive and nonaggressive groups which differed significantly from each other with subjects exposed to the aggressive models displaying the greater amount of aggression.

Influence of Sex of Model and Sex of Subjects on Imitation

The hypothesis that boys are more prone than girls to imitate aggression exhibited by a model was only partially confirmed. t tests computed for the subjects in the aggressive condition reveal that boys reproduced more imitative physical aggression than girls (t = 2.50 p < .01). The groups do not differ, however, in their imitation of verbal aggression.

The use of nonparametric tests, necessitated by the extremely skewed distributions of scores for subjects in the nonaggressive and control conditions, preclude an over-all test of the influence of sex of model per se, and of the various interactions between the main effects. Inspection of the means for subjects in the aggression condition, however, clearly suggests the possibility of a Sex x Model interaction. This interaction effect is much more consistent and pronounced for the male model than for the female model. Male subjects, for example, exhibited more physical (t = 2.07, p < .05) and verbal imitative aggression (t = 2.51, p < .05), more non-imitative aggression (t = 3.15, p < .025), and engaged in significantly more aggressive gun play (t = 2.12, p < .05) following exposure to the aggressive male model than the female subjects. In contrast, girls exposed to the female model performed considerably more imitative verbal aggression and more non-imitative aggression than did the boys. The variances, however, were equally large and with only a small N in each cell the mean differences did not reach statistical significance.

Data for the nonaggressive and control subjects provide additional suggestive evidence that the behavior of the male model exerted a greater influence than the female model on the subjects' behavior in the generalization situation.

It will be recalled that, except for the greater amount of mallet aggression exhibited by the control subjects, no significant differences were obtained between the nonaggressive and control groups. The data indicate, however, that the absence of significant differences between these two groups was due primarily to the fact that subjects exposed to the nonaggressive female model did not differ from the controls on any of the measures of aggression. With respect to the male model, on the other hand, the differences between the groups are striking. Comparison of the sets of scores by means of the sign test reveals that, in relation to the control group, subjects exposed to the nonaggressive male model performed significantly less imitative physical aggression (p = .06), less imitative verbal aggression (p = .002), less mallet aggression (p = .003), less nonimitative physical and verbal aggression (p = .03), and they were less inclined to punch the Bobo doll (p = .07).

While the comparison of subgroups, when some of the over-all tests do not reach statistical significance, is likely to capitalize on chance differences, nevertheless the consistency of the findings adds support to the interpretation in terms of influence by the model.

Nonaggressive Behavior

With the exception of expected sex differences, Lindquist (1956) Type III analyses of variance of the nonaggressive response scores yielded few significant differences.

Female subjects spent more time than boys playing with dolls (p < .001), with the tea set (p < .001), and coloring (p < .05). The boys, on the other hand, devoted significantly more time than the girls to exploratory play with the guns (p < .01). No sex differences were found in respect to the subjects use of the other stimulus objects, i.e., farm animals, cars, or tether ball.

Treatment conditions did produce significant differences on two measures of nonaggressive behavior that are worth mentioning. Subjects in the nonaggressive condition engaged in significantly more nonaggressive play with dolls than either subjects in the aggressive group (t = 2.67, p < .02), or in the control group (t = 2.57, p < .02).

Even more noteworthy is the finding that subjects who observed nonaggressive models spent more than twice as much time as subjects in aggressive condition (t = 3.07, p <.01) in simply sitting quietly without handling any of the play material.

DISCUSSION

Much current research on social learning is focused on the shaping of new behavior through rewarding and punishing consequences. Unless responses are emitted, however, they cannot be influenced. The results of this study provide strong evidence that observation of cues produced by the behavior of others is one effective means of eliciting certain forms of responses for which the original probability is very low or zero. Indeed, social imitation may hasten or short-cut the acquisition of new behaviors without the necessity of reinforcing successive approximations as suggested by Skinner (1953).

Thus subjects given an opportunity to observe aggressive models later reproduced a good deal of physical and verbal aggression (as well as nonaggressive responses) substantially identical with that of the model. In contrast, subjects who were exposed to nonaggressive models and those who had no previous exposure to any models only rarely performed such responses.

To the extent that observation of adult models displaying aggression communicates permissiveness for aggressive behavior, such exposure may serve to weaken inhibitory responses and thereby to increase the probability of aggressive reactions to subsequent frustrations. The fact, however, that subjects expressed their aggression in ways that clearly resembled the novel patterns exhibited by models provides striking evidence for the occurrence of learning by imitation.

In the procedure employed by Miller and Dollard (1941) for establishing imitative behavior, adult or peer models performed discrimination responses following which they were consistently rewarded, and the subjects were similarly reinforced whenever, matched the leaders' choice responses. While these experiments have been widely accepted as demonstrations of learning by means of imitation, in fact, they simply involve a special case of discrimination learning in which the behavior of others serves as discriminative stimuli for responses that are already part of the subject's repertoire. Auditory or visual environmental cues could easily have been substituted for the social stimuli to facilitate the discrimination learning. In contrast, the process of imitation studied in the present experiment differed in several important respects from the one investigated by Miller and Dollard in that subjects learned to combine fractional responses into relatively complex novel patterns solely by observing the performance of social models without any opportunity to perform the models' behavior m the exposure setting, and without any reinforcers delivered either to the models or to the observers.

An adequate theory of the mechanisms underlying imitative learning is lacking. The explanations that have been offered (Logan, Olmsted,

Rosner, Schwartz, & Stevens, 1955; Maccoby, 1959) assume that the imitator performs the model's responses covertly. If it can be assumed additionally that rewards and punishments are self-administered in conjunction with the covert responses, the process of imitative learning could be accounted for in terms of the same principles that govern instrumental trial-and-error learning. In the early stages of the developmental process, however, the range of component responses in the organism's repertoire is probably increased through a process of classical conditioning (Bandura & Huston,; 1961; Mowrer, 1950).

The data provide some evidence that the male model influenced the subjects' behavior outside the exposure setting to a greater extent than was true for the female model. In the analyses of the Sex x Model interactions, for example, only the comparisons involving the male model yielded significant differences. Similarly, subjects exposed to the nonaggressive male model performed less aggressive behavior than the controls, whereas comparisons involving the female model were consistently nonsignificant.

In a study of learning by imitation, Rosenblith (1959) has likewise found male experimenters more effective than females in influencing childrens' behavior. Rosenblith advanced the tentative explanation that the school setting may involve some social deprivation in respect to adult males which, in turn, enhances the male's reward value.

The trends in the data yielded by the present study suggest an alternative explanation. In the case of a highly masculine-typed behavior such as physical aggression, there is a tendency for both male and female subjects to imitate the male model to a greater degree than the female model. On the other hand, in the case of verbal aggression, which is less clearly sex linked, the greatest amount of imitation occurs in relation to the same-sex model. These trends together with the finding that boys in relation to girls are in general more imitative of physical aggression but do not differ in imitation of verbal aggression, suggest that subjects may be differentially affected by the sex of the model but that predictions must take into account the degree to which the behavior in question is sex-typed.

The preceding discussion has assumed that maleness-femaleness rather than some other personal characteristics of the particular models involved, is the significant variable -- an assumption that cannot be tested directly with the data at hand. It was clearly evident, however, particularly from boys' spontaneous remarks about the display of aggression by the female model, that some subjects at least were responding in terms of a sex discrimination and their prior learning about what is sex appropriate behavior (e.g., "Who is that lady. That's not the way for a lady to behave. Ladies are supposed to act like ladies. . ." "You should have seen what that girl did in there. She was just acting like a man. I never saw a girl act like that before. She was punching and fighting but no swearing."). Aggression by the male model, on the other hand, was more likely to be seen as appropriate and approved by both the boys ("Al's a good socker, he beat up Bobo. I want to sock like Al.") and the girls ("That man is a strong fighter, he punched and punched and he could hit Bobo right down to the floor and if Bobo got up he said, 'Punch your nose.' He's a good fighter like Daddy.").

The finding that subjects exposed to the quiet models were more inhibited and unresponsive than subjects in the aggressive condition, together with the obtained difference on the aggression measures, suggests that exposure to inhibited models not only decreases the probability of occurrence of aggressive behavior but also generally restricts the range of behavior emitted by the subjects.

"Identification with aggressor" (Freud, 1946) or "defensive identification" (Mowrer, 1950), whereby a person presumably transforms himself from object to agent of aggression by adopting the attributes of an aggressive threatening model so as to allay anxiety, is widely accepted as an explanation of the imitative learning of aggression.

The development of aggressive modes of response by children of aggressively punitive adults, however, may simply reflect object displacement without involving any such mechanism of defensive identification. In studies of child training antecedents of aggressively antisocial adolescents (Bandura & Walters, 1959) and of young hyper aggressive boys (Bandura, 1960), the parents were found to be non-permissive and punitive of aggression directed toward themselves. On the other hand, they actively encouraged and reinforced their sons aggression toward persons outside the home. This pattern of differential reinforcement of aggressive behavior served to inhibit the boys' aggression toward the original instigators and fostered the displacement of aggression toward objects and situations eliciting much weaker inhibitory responses.

Moreover, the findings from an earlier study (Bandura & Huston, 1961), in which children imitated to an equal degree aggression exhibited by a nurturant and a nonnurturant model, together with the results of the present experiment in which subjects readily imitated aggressive models who were more or less neutral figures suggest that mere observation of aggression, regardless of the quality of the model-subject relationship, is a sufficient condition for producing imitative aggression in children. A comparative study of the subjects' imitation of aggressive models who are feared, who are liked and esteemed, or who are essentially neutral figures would throw some light on whether or not a more parsimonious theory than the one involved in "identification with the aggressor" can explain the modeling process.

SUMMARY

Twenty-four preschool children were assigned to each of three conditions. One experimental group observed aggressive adult models; a second observed inhibited non-aggressive models; while subjects in a control group had no prior exposure to the models. Half the subjects in the experimental conditions observed same-sex models and hall viewed models of the opposite sex. Subjects were then tested for the amount of imitative as well as nonimitative aggression performed in a new situation in the absence of the models.

Comparison of the subjects' behavior in the generalization situation revealed that subjects exposed to aggressive models reproduced a good deal of aggression resembling that of the models, and that their mean scores differed markedly from those of subjects in the nonaggressive and control groups. Subjects in the aggressive condition also exhibited significantly more partially imitative and nonimitative aggressive behavior and were generally less inhibited in their behavior than subjects in the nonaggressive condition.

Imitation was found to be differentially influenced by the sex of the model with boys showing more aggression than girls following exposure to the male model, the difference being particularly marked on highly masculine-typed behavior.

Subjects who observed the nonaggressive models, especially the subdued male model, were generally less aggressive than their controls.

The implications of the findings based on this experiment and related studies for the psychoanalytic theory of identification with the aggressor were discussed.

REFERENCES

BANDURA, A. Relationship of family patterns to behavior disorders. Progress Report, 1960, Stanford University, Project No. M-1734, United States Public Health Service.

BANDURA, A., & HUSTON, ALETHA C. Identification as a process of incidental learning. J. abnorm. soc. Psychol., 1961, 63, 311-318.

BANDURA, A., & WALTERS, R. H. Adolescent aggression. New York: Ronald, 1959.

BLAKE, R. R. The other person in the situation. In R. Tagiuri & L. Petrullo (Eds.), Person perception and interpersonal behavior. Stanford, Calif: Stanford Univer. Press, 1958. Pp. 229-242.

FAULS, LYDIA B., & SMITH, W. D. Sex-role learning of five-year olds. J. genet. Psychol., 1956, 89, 105-117

FREUD, ANNA. The ego and the mechanisms of defense. New York: International Univer. Press, 1946.

GROSSER, D., POLANSKY, N., & LIPPIT, R. A laboratory study of behavior contagion. Hum. Relat 1951, 4, 115-142.

LINDQUIST, E. F. Design and analysis of experiments. Boston: Houghton Mifflin, 1956.

LOGAN, F., OLMSTED, O. L., ROSNER, B. S., SHWARTZ, R. D., & STEVENS, C. M. Behavior theory and social science. New Haven: Yale Univer. Press, 1955.

MACCOBY, ELANOR E. Role-taking in childhood and its consequences for social learning. Child Develpm., 1959, 30, 239-252.

MILLER, N. F., & DOLLARD, J. Social learning and imitation. New Haven: Yale Univer. Press, 1941.

MOWRER, O. H. (Ed.) Identification: A link between learning theory and psychotherapy. In, Learning theory and personality dynamics. New York: Ronald, 1950. Pp.69-94.

ROSENBAUM, M. E., & DERCHARMS, R. Direct and vicarious reduction of hostility. J. abnorm. soc. Psychol., 1960, 60, 105-111.

ROSENBLITH, JUDY F. Learning by imitation in kindergarten children. Child Develpm., 1959, 30, 69-80.

SCHACTER, S., & HALL, R. Group-derived restraints and audience persuasion. Hum. Relat., 1952, 5, 397-406.

SKINNER, B. F. Science and human behavior. New York: Macmillan, 1953.

LEARN MORE

To learn more about Albert Bandura's ground-breaking Bobo Doll experiment, visit the following link to listen to an excellent BBC radio broadcast on the subject presented by Claudia Hammond.

www.bbc.co.uk/programmes/b008fxv9

3. READ MORE PSYCHOLOGY CLASSICS

Conditioned Emotional Reactions: The Case of Little Albert

Conditioned Emotional Reactions by John B. Watson and Rosalie Rayner is one of the most influential, infamous and iconic research articles ever published in the history of psychology. Commonly referred to as "The Case of Little Albert" this psychology classic attempted to show how fear could be induced in an infant through classical conditioning. Originally published in 1920, Conditioned Emotional Reactions remains among the most frequently cited journal articles in introductory psychology courses and textbooks.

One of the most dramatic aspects of Watson and Rayner's original study was that they had planned to test a number of methods by which they could remove Little Albert's conditioned fear responses. However, as Watson noted "Unfortunately Albert was taken from the hospital the day the above tests were made. Hence the opportunity of building up an experimental technique by means of which we could remove the conditioned emotional responses was denied us."

This unforeseen turn of events was something that obviously stayed with Watson, as under his guidance some three years later, Mary Cover Jones conducted a follow-up study - A Laboratory Study of Fear: The Case of Peter - which illustrated how fear may be removed under laboratory conditions. This additional and highly relevant article is also presented in full.

You can get hold of Conditioned Emotional Reactions: The Case of Little Albert via the following Amazon website link.

www.amazon.com/dp/B00BOVL3TQ

Significant Aspects of Client-Centered Therapy

Widely regarded as one of the most influential psychologists of all time, Carl Rogers was a towering figure within the humanistic movement towards person centered theory and non-directive psychotherapy.

Originally published in 1946 his classic article Significant Aspects of Client-Centered Therapy is essential reading for anybody interested in psychotherapy and counseling. In this landmark publication Carl Rogers outlines the origins of client-centered therapy, the process of client-centered therapy, the discovery and capacity of the client and the client-centered nature of the therapeutic relationship.

Significant Aspects of Client-Centered Therapy builds upon some of Carl Rogers' previously published work. Among the most notable of these earlier articles were The Processes of Therapy and The Development of Insight in A Counseling Relationship; both of which are also presented in full.

You can get hold of Significant Aspects of Client-Centered Therapy via the following Amazon website link.

www.amazon.com/dp/B00BSY6WGI

Hierarchy of Needs: A Theory of Human Motivation

A Theory of Human Motivation by Abraham H. Maslow is one of the most famous psychology articles ever written. Originally published in 1943, it was in this landmark paper that Maslow presented his first detailed representation of Self-Actualization - the desire to become everything that one is capable of becoming - at the pinnacle of a hierarchy of human needs.

In A Theory of Human Motivation Maslow draws upon some of his earlier published work. Three of these key references, Conflict, Frustration And The Theory of Threat, The Dynamics of

Psychological Security-Insecurity and Preface To Motivation Theory are also presented in full.

You can get hold of Hierarchy of Needs: A Theory of Human Motivation via the following Amazon website link.

www.amazon.com/dp/B004JKMUKU

4. CONNECT AND LEARN

Join thousands of psychology enthusiasts online.

Psychology on Facebook

www.facebook.com/psychologyonline

Psychology on Twitter

twitter.com/psych101

Psychology on Google+

goo.gl/hU8JL

Psychology on Linkedin

www.linkedin.com/groups/Psychology-Students-Network-4016322/about

Psychology on YouTube

www.youtube.com/user/LearnAboutPsychology

Psychology on Pinterest

pinterest.com/psychology

Psychology Student Guide

The Psychology Student Guide is designed for anyone who would like to learn more about what psychology actually is; anyone who is thinking about studying the subject or anyone who is currently a psychology student. See following Amazon website link for full details.

www.amazon.com/dp/B009ZC2UOS

The "ALL ABOUT" Website Portfolio

www.all-about-psychology.com

www.all-about-forensic-psychology.com

www.all-about-forensic-science.com

www.all-about-body-language.com

Printed in Great Britain
by Amazon.co.uk, Ltd.,
Marston Gate.